STATEMENT

OF

FACTS

RESPECTING THE

EVERSDEN

ENCLOSURE BILLS.

—————

F. HODSON, PRINTER, CAMBRIDGE.

STATEMENT,

&c.

--------◦◦◦◦◦--------

IN the month of August, 1809, Lord Hardwicke wrote to the Dean of Carlisle on the subject of enclosing the parishes of Great and Little Eversden, expressing his hope of obtaining the concurrence of Queen's College, of whose estate he is the lessee, and communicating his intention of directing the usual notices to be placed on the church doors, in order to enable the proprietors to apply to Parliament. To this letter the following answer was received:

Carlisle Deanery, 26th August, 1809.

MY LORD,

Though I do not remember with any degree of precision what I said in that answer to your Lordship about two years ago, to which you now refer, I feel assured that I could not do otherwise than express both my own entire disposition, as well as that of the College, to accord with your Lordship's wishes whenever it should be in our power to do so: neither at present can I have the least difficulty in repeating the same sentiments. At the same time I think it but right to inform your Lordship, that the expences of some enclosures in which the College have been concerned, have proved so very unexpected and enormous, as to make the Society at present in no very good humour in general with Commissioners, Surveyors, &c. and also disposed to receive their reports and promises with considerable reserve.

I need not tell your Lordship that a Master and Fellows of a College are beings whose interests have no sort of connexions with those of their successors; and therefore it is hardly to be expected that they should be ready to sacrifice present emoluments for the sake of future prospects, with the same cheerfulfulness as owners in fee simple may do. And further, we are not without suspicion that our fair interests have not always been attended to.

Still your Lordship will please not to understand me as opposing in any degree your Lordship's proposal, but merely as making you aware, that as every College act is that of the Master and majority of Fellows, how very necessary it is become that, as Master, I should guard against pledging the College upon any imperfect information. I hope to be in college in October next, and shall be happy to learn from Mr. Pemberton all the circumstances, and to find that the Master and Fellows can with propriety contribute to promote your Lordship's views. The Fellows, I doubt not, will have the same sentiments. When your Lordship recollects that for the space of more than thirty years last past I have on every occasion, without exception, exerted myself to oblige your Lordship and your Lordship's connexions, you will the more readily believe that, in hinting at some difficulties, I do not indulge the least of a cavilling spirit.

I am, always,

Your Lordship's most faithful servant,

ISAAC MILNER.

The Earl of Hardwicke.

At the latter end of March copies of the following printed letter were sent to the Tutors of several Colleges in Cambridge, and some of them were sent by the Solicitor of Queen's College to different Members of Parliament who had been educated at the University.

> Queen's Coll. Lodge, Cambridge,
> March 24, 1810.

The subject on which I venture to trouble you is to me very unpleasant; but the interests of Queen's College, over which I have the honour to preside, compel me, in conjunction with the Fellows of the College, to oppose the two Bills, now before Parliament, for inclosing the parishes of Great and Little Eversden, in the county of Cambridge.

This business is to me particularly unpleasant, because Lord Hardwicke, the principal promoter of the Bills, is a member of Queen's College, and because during the greater part of my life, and on some very important occasions, I have uniformly exerted myself to promote his Lordship's wishes.

But on the present occasion, according to the *very best* and *most perfectly unbiassed judgment* that I am able to exercise, I find it impossible to comply with the proposals of his Lordship's agents, consistently with the discharge of my duty to Queen's College.

It is true, that Lord Hardwicke applied to me by letter on the subject of the enclosures in the course of last summer; and it is also true, that since that time his Lordship has made various communications to me and to the College, partly by himself and partly by his principal agent, Christopher Pemberton, Esq; who is his Lordship's solicitor.

The answers to these communications, whether in

writing, or in conversations with Mr. Pemberton, have constantly expressed a disposition both in the Master and in the Fellows of the College to oblige his Lordship, and comply with his wishes as far as they could consistently with a due regard to the interests of Queen's College; but so far from going beyond these general expressions of civility, and of disposition to oblige Lord Hardwicke, the Master of Queen's College, with the concurrence of the Fellows, has constantly guarded against even the remotest idea that the College had committed themselves on this subject; and moreover, when pressed to appoint a Commissioner, the Master in particular, has always declined the appointing of one, urging that as yet the College had by no means got *so far* in the business; and his language has constantly been that the College could not agree *to inclose at all*, unless they could obtain more precise views than they had hitherto been able to obtain, *as to the consequences and effects* of the intended inclosures.

Very little has been done, and certainly nothing satisfactory, to remove the doubts and difficulties which the College have felt respecting this matter; and, moreover, a variety of circumstances have taken place in the conduct of the promoters of these Bills, which have much increased the said doubts and difficulties, have served to put the College more on their guard, and determined them to oppose the present application to Parliament for the inclosure of the parish or parishes in question.

They observe, 1. That if notices were really put on the church doors of Great and Little Eversden, of intended applications to Parliament for inclosing the two parishes, the College had no regular information respecting that step, and they certainly never approved of it.

2. The College never saw the Heads of the Bills, much less the printed copies of them, before they were presented to Parliament; nor to this moment have they seen the printed copies unless by a mere accident.

3. A Commissioner has been named for the College in the Bills without their leave or concurrence.

4. The College are Lords of the Manor of both the Eversdens; and they submit, whether, *under such circumstances*, the present Bills ought to pass.

5. Moreover, the parishes of Great and Little Eversden are so contiguous, and the lands so inter-mixed, that, supposing other difficulties could be got over, the enormous expence of *two Bills* forms an insuper-able objection. Great Eversden is supposed to contain not more than about 1000 statute acres of open land, and Little Eversden not more than 670, to be inclosed. The two parishes actually adjoin each other; and the farmers in both exercise a right of common and of sheep-walk together; so that the inclosing of Great Eversden ONLY would almost ruin the parish of Little Eversden.

6. Add, that as far as myself (the Master) and the Fellows of the College have been able to obtain in-formation, we understand that *many*, if *not most*, of the proprietors are absolutely averse to the inclosures.

7. And in regard to Queen's College it is to be observed, that as our lands already lie very much together, and in large pieces, and as we have the principal sheep-walk, there is little probability of our estate being improved by inclosing, unless some just and reasonable stipulations can be previously secured to the College, so that their present advantages may

not be left at large to the judgment of Commissioners. Then, besides these reasons for securing previous stipulations in favour of the College, the Master and Fellows could suggest *others*, and those very *material ones*, for the same purpose.

8. Mr. Pemberton has solicited the Bills, and a previous survey has been made under his direction, as we suppose; and this without the approbation or leave of the College and other proprietors; and thus the chief promoters of these Bills have ascertained the property of the proprietors without their knowledge.

9. A similar line of conduct has been pursued in regard to the intended inclosure of Kingston, in this county, where Queen's College has also a very considerable share of property : and I may add, that it merited consideration, whether all the three contiguous parishes, viz. Kingston and the two Eversdens, might not be joined in one Bill with advantage and propriety.

10. It must seem extraordinary, that Mr. Custance should be mentioned in the printed Bill as Commissioner for the Rector* of Little Eversden, whereas the Rector himself nominated Mr. Truslove.—N. B. Queen's College presents to this rectory; and the Rev. Mr. Heaton, the rector, has signed the petitions against the Bills.

11. As Master or President of Queen's College, I do earnestly request you, on the part of the said Master and the Fellows of the same, to give your serious attention to these Bills of Inclosure now before Parliament, and also to the petition of Queen's College against the said Bills. At present we are not so informed as to be sure that, under any circumstances,

---

* The Rector has signed the two petitions against the two Bills.

the College would be desirous of the proposed inclosures; and most certainly not according to the plan
of the present Bills, which have been hurried forward
in a most extraordinary manner, so as to give no
proper time for inquiry and deliberation.

Your very humble servant,

ISAAC MILNER,

President of Queen's College, Cambridge.

As soon as Lord Hardwicke was informed of the
circulation of the above paper, he wrote the following
letter to the Master of Queen's:

(Copy.)

St. James's Square, April 2d, 1810.

DEAR SIR,

I regret to find that you have sent through
the Tutors of the different colleges a circular letter to
such of their Members as are in Parliament, with a
view of engaging their opposition to the Eversden
Enclosure Bill. If this step had been taken in consequence of the failure of any attempt to remove the
doubts and difficulties which you state the college to
have felt respecting this matter, it would have been
perfectly natural; but, as I have never entertained a
wish to obtain the enclosure of the parish of Eversden,
or of any other in which I have property, in a manner
that would improve my estate at the expence of others,
or to the injury of any individual whatever, I should
have been at all times most anxious to obviate any
objections which the college might feel, and to go as
far as possible in conceding to their wishes. As the
printed letter contains several observations upon the
Eversden Enclosure, I think it better for the sake of

clearness to apply such answers as arise upon each in the order in which they stand, than to enter into any general detail upon the subject.

1. Having applied to the Master of Queen's about three years ago on the subject of the Enclosure of Eversden, and having then stated that notices would be placed upon the church door in August and September, in order to enable the parties to apply to Parliament if the measure should be subsequently agreed upon, I did not conceive the putting up of notices for the same purpose last summer could have been deemed in any manner disrespectful towards the college, being merely a provisional step, attended with no expence, and not pledging any person to support the measure; and the circumstance was, I believe, explained in my letter to you written last year. At all events I conceived the reason for that step was fully understood, as it is evident that no Bill of Enclosure can be brought in, unless notices are placed on the church door and inserted in the newspapers in the months of August and September preceding the Session of Parliament.

2. It never could be intended to conceal from the college the Heads of the Bill, as it was both the desire and interest of myself and every other proprietor, to obtain the concurrence of the college, not only to the measure in general, but to the particular details of it.*

3. The order of the House of Commons now requires that all private bills should be presented on an early day in the session; and the name of Mr. Truslove was inserted as the Commissioner for the college, for no other reason than because from his

---

* The usual mode of communicating Bills to the Proprietors, is to circulate prints of the Bills, and copies were sent to the College within a very few days after the Bill was printed.

having been employed by the college upon this business, and being constantly in the habit of acting as a Commissioner, it was thought that he would be the person whom the college would prefer upon this occasion. If, however, any circumstance should induce them to wish that some other person should be named, it can be altered without any difficulty.

4. This article states, that "the college submit, "whether under the circumstance of their being Lords "of the Manor of Great and Little Eversden, the "Bills ought to pass." If it appears that the rights of the Lords of the Manor are likely to be infringed, or their property injured in value, it is undoubtedly a reason for an opposition to the Bill, but the mere circumstance of the college being Lords of the Manor is not of itself a reason against the passing of the Bill.* I take the fact to be, that by the improvement of the estates situated in Eversden the value of the copyholds will be considerably encreased; and as I understand they are held at fine arbitrary, the College Estate will of course be proportionably benefitted by the improvement which will immediately arise from dividing and allotting the lands now dispersed over the common fields, and this without any expence to the College.

5. It would certainly have been desirable to have included the parishes of Great and Little Eversden in

---

* It would be in many cases highly unjust, if the Lord of the Manor had the power of putting a veto on the passing of an Enclosure Bill. There is a large parish near Cambridge where the Lord of the Manor has no property in land, and if the proprietors should wish to have their lands laid together, there could be no reason for objecting to such division and allotment, unless they attempted to infringe on the rights of the Lord of the Manor. In the case of Eversden, the proportion of waste is not considerable, but whatever it may be, the college would have the usual proportion in such cases.

the same Bill, and this was my wish, if Mr. Pemberton could have come to an understanding with the College before the time appointed by the House of Commons for receiving private Bills. But I apprehend the saving of Parliamentary charges would have been very inconsiderable, though in the making of fences, and in other subsequent and incidental expences, there might have been a saving both of trouble and expence. But as I shall give up the Enclosure of Little Eversden if the College are averse to it, the bringing in of separate Bills became unavoidable: if, however, the College can be reconciled to the enclosure of both parishes, I hope and believe the Bills may yet be united for every practical purpose of convenience and œconomy, in carrying the measure into effect.

6. I have not received any representations from any of the proprietors against the enclosure, though it is extremely possible that there may be some to whom the immediate expence will be inconvenient, notwithstanding the permanent improvement of the property by laying the lands in severalty.

7. So far as I am personally concerned I cannot be averse to any proposals that are just and reasonable; and as so many parishes in Cambridgeshire, including the estates of many of the colleges, have been enclosed within the last twenty years, there can be no difficulty in ascertaining what the practice has been in cases similar to the present.

8. I was not aware that any objection had been made to Mr. Pemberton being Solicitor of the Bill. I believe there is no one of his profession who has had more experience upon the subject, or who would execute the duty with more integrity and ability. With respect

to the survey, I had no other view in desiring it to be made, than to enable the Commissioners to proceed to the execution of their trust as soon as possible after the passing of the Act, in order that each proprietor might have his allotment in the ensuing Autumn. This advantage, which, in all cases of enclosure is a very great one, cannot be obtained unless the map is ready soon after the passing of the Act. If the Commissioners have any desire to ascertain the correctness of the survey, they can easily verify it before they proceed to act upon it. In the mean time I beg leave to state, that the sole motive I had in view in incurring the expence of the survey, was to promote the general convenience of all parties.

9. The parish of Kingston is for the most part already enclosed; the open field amounting to about 900 acres, over which I have a right of sheep-walk. This open field lies between the enclosed part, which is my property, and the village, and I was not aware that any objection could be made to my undertaking, at my own risque, the expence of the survey of the above quantity of open field, over which I have a right of sheep-walk, and in which I have considerable property.* I am not aware that the enclosure of Kingston could have been united with the Bill for enclosing the two Eversdens.

10. I am not enabled to explain the matter stated in this article.†

---

* It has since appeared, that Mr. Custance was prevented by other engagements from entering upon the survey of this parish, so that no survey, in point of fact, has yet been made of the open field of Kingston.

† Mr. Truslove being named by the College as Lord of the Manor, could not be named for the Rector.

11. I was not aware, and am sorry to learn from this article, that the College have thought it right to present petitions against all the above Enclosure Bills of Great and Little Eversden and Kingston,‡ in which I happen to be concerned; nor am I at present informed on what grounds their objections rest, or by what means they could be removed. If I were so informed I trust I need not say that I should be ready to accede to any proposals which are just and reasonable, and I am confident the College would not ask or expect any that are not of that description, and which have not been usual in similar cases, when the interests of Colleges and of individuals are jointly concerned. Since the above was written I have received your letter of yesterday's date, explaining the circumstances which prevented you from sending me a copy of your printed letter. My reason for writing to Mr. Wood was, that having seen the copy which Lord Euston had received from Mr. Tavel, of Trinity, and another which had been sent to Sir James Hall, of Christ College, I took it for granted that the Tutor of St. John's would also be furnished with some copies for the same purpose, and under all the circumstances I was not sure how far you would like to be applied to for one on my behalf. It was not my intention, however, that Mr. Wood should apply to you upon the subject, and still less that you should have the trouble of entering into a detailed explanation of the circumstances which have engaged your time. I am to have the pleasure of seeing Mr. Harrison to-morrow morning, and shall be very happy if any mode can be devised to remove the objections which you have at present to the Eversden

‡ It appears the College have not petitioned against the enclosure of Kingston.

Enclosure Bill. In the mean time I flatter myself the observations which I have made upon the paragraphs of your printed letter, will explain to your satisfaction some of the points which appear to have been mis-understood, and I doubt not unintentionally, mis-construed.

I remain, dear Sir,
With great regard,
Your's, &c.
HARDWICKE.

On the 10th of April Lord Hardwicke had a meet-ing with the Dean of Carlisle at Queen's Lodge, in the presence of Mr. Harrison, one of the Fellows of the College. At this interview the Master said, that the only point of real importance was, that the Com-missioners to whom the charge of laying in severalty the lands of the different proprietors now dispersed over the common fields should be committed, should be men of judgment, experience, and integrity; and that if Lord Hardwicke would agree to the nomination of a third Commissioner instead of the person who had been named by the proprietors at large, there would be no further objection on the part of the College to the enclosure of Great and Little Eversden.

On this basis the following articles were proposed by the Dean of Carlisle :—

1. On the supposition that all three are to be in one Bill, then, Truslove, Custance, Wedge, without saying who is who; in case of death of any one, his place to be supplied by the proprietors at large.

2. A Surveyor to be named in the Act, independent of them all, (Qy. Watford or Collinson,) and the pre-sent survey, made by Mr. Custance at the expence of Lord Hardwicke, to be given up.

3. To ascertain, previously to the Committee, whether the Sequestrator of Great Eversden chuses to commute his Vicarial Tithes; and if he does, then to have a clause settling the proportion of land between the Lay-impropriator and the Sequestrator, to be given in lieu of tithes.

Article 3. is founded on a memorandum given by Mr. Truslove to the Master, " That there be a previous " clause in the Act for the division of tithes between " the Lay-impropriator of Great Eversden and the " Sequestrator of Great Eversden."

4. The clause (p. 11.) in the Great Eversden Bill as to the moiety of glebe, to remain as it is now in the Bill.

As there were many objections to including the Kingston Enclosure Bill in that for the Enclosure of Great and Little Eversden, particularly from the difficulty of persuading the proprietors to give up the Commissioner whom they had chosen at a publick meeting held for that purpose, Lord Hardwicke thought it right to state the following questions to the Dean of Carlisle, in order that he might be prepared to explain distinctly the wishes and intention of the College to a meeting of the smaller proprietors of Eversden, appointed for that day :—

1st. Question by Lord Hardwicke.—Supposing Kingston to be in a separate Bill, and altogether distinct from the two Eversdens, would the College withdraw the consent they have given to the proceeding with the enclosure of the two latter parishes?

Answer.—Yes, we withdraw the consent as to Eversden being enclosed by the Commissioners above named.

2. Lord Hardwicke asked whether, in case, from any difficulty amongst the smaller proprietors of Kings-

ton, or from the forms of the House of Commons, it should be found impracticable to include Kingston in the same Bill with the two Eversdens, the Master and Fellows of Queen's College would in that case feel it necessary to oppose the enclosure of Eversden upon the terms stated above, in paragraphs 1, 2, 3, and 4?

Yes, and Kingston too.

3. Whether, if from the difficulty of including Kingston and the Eversdens in one Bill Lord Hardwicke withdraws the Kingston Enclosure Bill for this session, the College would then acquiesce in the enclosure of the two Eversdens, on the terms above stated?

No! objecting only to the Commissioners.

4. Question.—If Kingston cannot be so included, on what terms would the Master and Fellows of Queen's College consent to the enclosure of Eversdens?

Answer.—It depends on who are the Commissioners. Let them be as follows :—

For the Lay Impropriator, Custance.

Proprietors,.......... { The Reverend Mr. Heaton, of Little Eversden, to nominate one, subject to the approbation of Lord Hardwicke, as Lay Impropriator, or of the other propietors.

The Lord of the Manor, Truslove.

In consequence of the above suggestion, Lord Hardwicke endeavoured to persuade the proprietors of Eversden, assembled at the meeting at Arrington, to adopt the proposal recommended to them on the part of the College of considering the three Commissioners, Messrs. Truslove, Custance, and Dugmore, as Commissioners for the enclosure generally; and further explained to them, that in case of any of them declining or being unable to act, the vacancy was to be supplied by the proprietors at large. The result of the meeting was not such as Lord Hardwicke had hoped it might have been, the proprietors declining to change the Commissioner whom they had elected at a publick meeting appointed for that purpose, and chosen, as they unanimously asserted, without any influence having been used with them, or any the slightest suggestion having been made from any quarter of any particular person. The question being thus reduced to the single point of whether Mr. Dugmore or Mr. Thorpe, both understood to be respectable and experienced men in the line of their profession, should be the Commissioner for the smaller proprietors, it was not unreasonable to hope, that the College would feel it unnecessary to persist in their opposition to the Bill; and it was in the view of expressing the above hope, and also of ascertaining their further intentions, that the following letter was addressed to the Master immediately after the meeting.

Wimpole, April 10, 1810.

MY DEAR SIR,

As Mr. Hunt and Mr. Finch will have informed you generally of what passed at the meeting at Arrington, I can only say that I regret very sincerely that the attempt which I made to conciliate the smaller proprietors of Eversden to the proposal suggested by you on the part of the College, to adopt the nomination of Mr. Dugmore instead of Mr. Thorpe, was not more successful.

Mr. Truslove was mentioned at the meeting by Mr. Hunt, as a Commissioner for the College; Mr. Dugmore was proposed by Mr. Heaton. as Rector of Little Eversden, on the idea of uniting the two Bills; and Mr. Custance, as Commissioner on my part, as

Impropriator. This was stated before the smaller proprietors came into the room; when I represented to them the expediency of coming to an amicable understanding before the discussion of the Bill in Parliament, and recommended to them in this view to accept of the above gentlemen as Commissioners for the enclosure generally, without considering them as named by any particular interests. When this question was put to the vote, they all, with the exception of Mr. Marshall, persisted in retaining Mr. Thorpe, who had been nominated as their Commissioner at a meeting called for that purpose. After the endeavours I have used with the most sincere anxiety to bring this business to an amicable termination, in the manner which appeared most agreeable to yourself and the College, I still hope that you will not feel it necessary to oppose the measure. I had promised Lord Euston, who was desirous of going out of town, that the Bill should not be read a second time till after this week; but on account of the Easter recess, which will take place on Thursday se'nnight, it will be necessary it should be read a second time on Monday or Tuesday next. The proprietors of Little Eversden are very anxious that the enclosure of that parish should proceed at the same time with the enclosure of Great Eversden; but unless the College consents, of course no alteration will be made in respect to the tithes. I return to London to-morrow morning, and shall be much obliged to you for a few lines directed to St. James's Square.

I am, dear Sir,

With great regard,

Your obedient and faithful servant,

HARDWICKE.

The Rev. the Dean of Carlisle.

Queen's Lodge, 13th April, 1810.

MY LORD,

A meeting of two or three Syndicates, also a Congregation yesterday and another to-day, have prevented me from writing.

Yet I have found time to read over your Lordship's letter more than twenty times; and Mr. Harrison will have told you how confounded I was on reading it at first, and also how really blind I was to its real meaning. I cannot understand what sort of answer your Lordship can expect me to give under all the circumstances: however, as soon as it is in my power, I will endeavour to write more at length.

I am, my Lord,
Your Lordship's obedient servant,
I. MILNER.

Earl of Hardwicke.

If it should appear that the Bill contains any provisions which are not usually inserted in Bills of this description, or that any advantages which have ever been given by express enactment, in cases where College interests have been concerned, can be given to Queen's College upon this occasion, the promoters of the Bill have never been unwilling to submit to any proper alterations. Having understood, originally, that the objection of the College was founded principally on the apprehension of the expences frequently occasioned by Acts of Enclosure, Lord Hardwicke offered to remove that objection by engaging to defray the whole expence that might be chargeable upon the College Estate, if the College would agree to grant the next renewal of the Lease (of which there are 19 years from Michaelmas last) without any encrease of the fine, in consequence of the improvement occasioned by the expence of the Enclosure. By this proposal he is still willing to abide; and being aware that a College cannot legally bind their successors, he has always professed himself ready to accept as an engagement, a declaration of the opinion of the present members of the society, of the equity of such an agreement, recorded on the minutes of the College.

April 26, 1810.

POSTSCRIPT.
April 28, 1810.

Since the above statement was printed, a second paper has been published by the Master of Queen's College, in which all the objections of the former letter are again urged, and with encreased asperity.—There is also an insinuation respecting a *specious* negociation, which I consider so extremely unjust and injurious, that it will require some further observations; more especially, as what passed at the meeting of the proprietors at Arrington, is either entirely misrepresented or perverted.

HARDWICKE.

FINIS.

[HODSON, PRINTER, CAMBRIDGE.